THE ANGEL
OF DEATH
IN THE
ADONIS
LOUNGE

poems by

Marc Almond

Gay Verse from GMP — The Gay Men's Press

This edition first published in March 1988
by GMP Publishers Ltd., P O Box 247, London N15 6RW, England
Collection world copyright © 1988 GMP Publishers Ltd
Poems world copyright © 1988 Marc Almond

Distributed in North America by
Alyson Publications Inc.,
40 Plympton Street, Boston, MA 02118, USA
telephone: (617) 542 5679

British Library Cataloguing in Publication Data

Almond, Marc
  The angel of death in the Adonis lounge
  I.Title
  821'.914

ISBN 0-85449-079-5

Photo of Marc Almond by Andrew Catlin
Illustrations by 'Red Hot Johnny'

Printed and bound in the European Community
by Nørhaven A/S, Viborg, Denmark

Preface

The Angel of Death in the Adonis Lounge is Marc Almond's first published collection of poems.

The versatile and unique talent of Marc Almond is never better exemplified than in this collection of verse and poetry. I doubt very much that many of the public would appreciate his poetry to the full, regarding him as an eccentric singer and performer rather than a poet; but the selection presented here offers a representative range of his work in all its varied moods. The wry, even sick sense of the absurd through to the sense of enchanted stasis and onwards, reveals a personal complexity that remains intellectually rigorous.

Marc Almond, espying and revealing, uses a purposely idiosyncratic voice to accost the reader. He is equally tough, pragmatic, and beneath it all deeply satirical. His tone is concerned, at once alarming, inventive and purposely uncomfortable.

His world, and the world of his writing is like no other.

Mark Langthorne

The following words and verse were written between the years 1980-87. They are explorations and observations, they part document my ever changing attitudes. I would like to thank Stephen Maxwell and Mark Langthorne for helping me to assemble this collection, and for tidying my ragged edges.

I dedicate the book to some people who have stood by me through the stormy years — Jane Rollink, Huw Feather, Annie Hogan, Stevo, Anita Sarko, Liz Pugh, Mark Langthorne, and all of my most loyal of fans. A special thanks to the Gay Men's Press.

Thank you to Warner Music for the kind use of *Saint Judy* and *The Hustler*.

I remain a sensualist and adventurer.

Marc Almond 1987

Contents

Lonely, Lonely

Send me blue dahlias:
A bucket of spit
To moisten the slick of your thighs.

Sexual adventurer,
Sexual animal,
Prowler through darkness
Sleepwalker, predator.
Lonely kisses
Nameless minutes,
Lonely, lonely
Sexual animal.
Somnambulist, drifter
Haunting the West Side.
Hunter explorer,
Prowler through the world,
Under the world.
Where is your fire?
Aching, awaking,
In slumbersome tread,
Emissary from death
Watching over your shoulder,
Halo of dread,
Danger on lips
In the velour of night.

Lonely, lonely
Sexual animal
Hunter and hunted,
Taking shapes
Until morning,
Repeatedly appearing
Tireless, faceless,
Jaded, endless.

Be somebody else,
Be anyone else,
Be nameless
Blameless
Wantonly shameless.

Drifter in dreamland
Naked in your sorrow,
There's danger on lips
In deep velvet of night.

Lonely, lonely,
Lonely, lonely
Aching, aching...

Love Amongst the Ruined

So OK
You think I'm some kind of
Semolina-headed
Fired and fettered
Little virgin
Well, that's OK with me
One arm in the ashtray
One arm round your neck
Pulling you across the six-week sheets to me
Oh! You see
I could be a walking one-man career
For some psychiatrist
It's true,
I'm open to everyone
Unique to few.
What about you?
Yeah! What about you?
A sleaze burger
Grease grimer
Eyeliner
Whiner:
Up to your ears in a mecca of broken dreams.
Only just getting by
With another calculated lie.
Your lobotomy eyes
Tell me a million different versions
Of what you've been
And what you've seen
Trying to dodge the shadows
Of the lights upon the tarmac.
Desperation kicks me to the kill.
But baby!
I'm waiting at the station
For my train to ruination
Just trying to find a way to cheat the bill.
If they hit you on one cheek
Then smash them on the other,
It's a knuckle-duster path
We walk to survive.

Pinch myself and shake the sand out of the seams,
Until the time
To climb out of the litter bin arrives.
Loose limbed and lycra lipped
My lipsalve sticks on you
Blitzed and bomber bug eyes
Bite the soft skin on the inside
Resist the watering sensation
To bite my way right through.

All washed up and nowhere to go
All washed up and nowhere to go
Nowhere to go
To go.

The kitchen smell
All burnt and smoked up
Soaked up stale milk
Rotten peel across the floor.

Watch you with admiration
As you get yourself together,
To peel the damp dried
Teabags off the wall:
Salvage up some sugar
To sweeten up together,
From the bugs that bite
Escaping from the bed
Love this riddled ruin
Be the bag to hide my head in,
Or walk the weary way
To desolation day, instead
We're waiting at the station
For our train to ruination
Who cares the destination!
Who cares if we arrive!
The smell of us
The damp
That eats the bathroom round the tiles,
Something tells me
We've been here all the time.

The Angel of Death in the Adonis Lounge

The Angel of Death
In the Adonis Lounge,
Rock black nipples
And thick black prick
Damp from kissing mothers
In terminal labour,
Sweet and deadly,
Sarcastic and sad
And cocky with favours.

His smile sweetly crooked
And embrace softly violent.
Pupils are wide
And sockets empty.
Desperate eyes,
Beautiful.
Groin filled, but never yielding,
Marbled heart,
A garlanded grave.

He is as rich as hashish,
Exotic and brown,
Dark as the earth
Damp as the soil
Erotic and sweet,
Opiate, healer

Their breath in his mouth
Taking their souls to his lungs,
Their lives to his heart
Dusted with centuries' sighs,
He is the sombre promise,
Their retribution.
He is silent and beautiful
Silent and deadly.
He touches me.
I am his.
I am ...
I am ... gone.

Swinging the pendulum.
The clock stops.

Songs That Are Sung in the Night

Songs that are sung
    in the night
    are pitiful songs:
Themes for the lonely sleepless.
Woes to the blue of heart
Songs that are sung
    in the dark
Are haunted moans
For a hand in motion,
A mysterious song
For someone out there
    in the dark.
My room turns on me,
Walls creep to eat me,
My bed sucks me,
Vented, and shallow
Scented
Soured perspiration
Turns out to be made by me.

Untitled

And this precious jewel
I could give to you
Colour me red
When I'm feeling blue.
The colour of a kiss
In a young girl's dream,
The mark of the guillotine.

Grey Veil of September

Eyes blinding grey
Muggy veil of September
Rain beating down
On seamy streets of amber.
Storm coming down
And I'm feeling kinda lonely
Tenements brooding
Like hope that survives death.
Somewhere a battered radio
Croons a song of yesteryear,
Cracklin' interference
And the buzzin' of neon.
Stranger on the corner
Raises his collar,
Looks for a telephone;
And I'm trying to remember
To remember
To remember.

Eye blinding grey
Muggy veil of September,
Horses dying in the gutter,
In a fog of steamy colic.
Storm coming down
And I'm feeling kinda lonely
Me and some old sad affair
A painful pairing,
Autumn thorns
And hips and whores
'you can take me for a dollar.'
Fists that hammer on the walls
That keep me here a prisoner.
Gotta brave the rain
The heat of sticky grey September,
And I'm trying to remember
To remember
To remember.

All night and day
All day, night and day
A lamplight burns in my window:
Burns to keep away the phantoms
Making for my heart:
All night they howl, the wolves
Waiting on my sleeping
All night they laugh, the jackals
Looking for some empty cave
To live in.

And rain,
Splashing violently upon
The sighing pavestones,
Cleansing all the filth
And pent-up fury.
Crouched
And simmering,
Air eddies, like some undulating current
Wanting and waiting to pull me down
Pulsing full of memories that
Loiter round to meet me.
Veiled and grey as September.
The youth hangs round in doorways
Waiting eagerly for murder.
Storm coming down
And I'm feeling kinda lonely
Gonna murder your memory
Like you went and murdered mine
Somewhere a battered radio
Croons a song of yesteryear,
Songs that only go to fuel
My bile-embittered heartaches.
Gonna brave the rain and oppressive
Heat of sticky grey September
And I don't want to remember
To remember
To remember.

Untitled

The blue sky is scarred
With the trail of a plane,
Seems that God's
Cutting out thick white lines of cocaine.

Syph Gun and Taxi Cabs

On floors of dust we
Came
And went.
The hot euphoria,
Heaven sent.
And how we lived those times
Of riot,
Blue damnation cracked the quiet.
We used our dicks
To beat and stab,
Through syph
With gun
With taxi-cabs.
I gave you a ring of glass,
You thought you had the world.
I didn't sleep for nights
And nights
As though I'd killed someone.

Kip

Death wore his keys on
The right side
Visited the backrooms
The slicked-rim glory holes;
Dull ache of unrequited longing,
Shadows,
Drunken sailors...

...solid cold Kip
Selfish Kip
Kip grins
When all around him wanes
And wilts,
Like silken moons
Kip's pearled ass
Cheeks.
Kip's brutal stoned kisses
Lingering in the thickening air
Beats time for a million
Never nevers (those nights we howled
        in lonesome self-abuse)
On Kip spreadeagled
On a paisley bed.
Full glossed centrefold
Stick together my pages
Beautiful ruined Kip...

...death came
With shallow sorries,
Hollow goodbyes.
Left no name
No forwarding address
No date of birth
No gentle reminder for a card
At Christmas.
Death came wearing a black handkerchief
A yellow
A blue
A red for violent nights...

...Kip grinned,
Stoned:
Kip takes a stroll
Smokes some grass
Tight blue cutoffs
The tease of muscle
Taut ass.
The mischievous sunlight
Kisses the curves of Kip
Damped and hard,
Kissed by California's sun.
Kip smiles,
A smile to meet your thighs,
Thighs that soon
Would weld with his
Will wield like dreams' soft scythe:
Perfected form
Blessed form
Blessed with youth
Kip rolls his tongue,
His hips
His golden head from side to side,
Arches up
Hard and quick
Kip comes
From the wrist-thick dick.
Limb of countless steaming dreams
Dreams that weep
Of nights without sleep
The lonesome dreams of Kip.

The thing we want
So much to touch;
Our arms that want
So hard to hold
This vinyl Kip,
Beautiful frozen Kip,
Paper Kip
The pages will stick
And tear
Our perfect Kip.
But Kip drags
On the toke
And absorbs the gleam
Of the afternoon sun,
Those hard lines,
Those fruitful valleys
Of sickly Californian peach,
Sick California;
Sloppy molten kisses
Saturated denim by feverish
Desperate sweat.
For Kip never complains
About your imperfections,
Your small dick,
Your wasted chest.
Kip.
For castoffs, for the crippled,
That smiles that taunt
Yet illuminate,
The heaving
Swaying
Breathing backrooms
Of blind encounters.

Kip is God
In this Church
Of piss,
Of greased and grimy bodies,
Of spittled slippery palms.

Beautiful Kip
Is blind to this
The ugly shuffle
Of blind fish:
In a vacuous sucking
Lake of love;
Fingers that fumble for love,
The love that could be Kip's.
Kip's stoned love
And boy-blue eyes
Frozen ever more.
As Kip,
Shrivels and dies.
Frozen, down on you
He comes for you;
Seething, speechless, dead,
Of black rooms.
Blurred Adonis,
Of the anonymous mouth;
Ghostly flickering
Faceless studboy,
Of drooling
Cocained gums
Soured from late hours.
Pumping
On a slow loop,
For those that won't make
This dawn.
That die, as
The slow dumb
Smile of Kip
Who writes his name in pearl.
Those last drops
Of slow-motion Kip,

Wet with hair like a
Thousand golden whips,
And hips,
Like ships of seething seas
(For me)
And only me
Await
Empty
And dream of Kip.

Don't feel small when you
Gaze at Kip
Don't feel dried up
Tired and sick
(Sick you'll never have Kip)

Frustrated you'll never look
As lithe,
As tanned,
As young as Kip.
None of that soured old taste
For Kip,
Only the sweet tang of sorbet
And water-melon.

I feel a sadness
That haunts the lost backrooms,
Early mornings
Empty souls,
Rejected at my boiling points
Of desire;
The jaded hunter of a moment's
Warm need.
Embittered at the vibrant,
The glowing.
Sometimes.
Kill us with a wasting glance.

New York Poems

I The Crimson Diva

(for Miss Sarko)

Scintillating powdered crystal
Diamanté Deity,
Diva Anita
In her opium den.
Burnt orange,
Cats and roaches
Incense and dust
She nukes her face
With iridescence,
Purples, pink and gold,
On her
It's Christmas every day,
And the secrets of the Orient
Are in her cleavage.
Each evening she rises
From a pile of star-spangled clutter
Like a Royal Bag Lady
To roam the awed street
Of New York City.
Her night domain she rules.
(Tongues Hush)
The Crimson Diva comes.
What a woman!

II The Puerto Rican GoGo Boy

The Puerto Rican gogo boy
Gyrates in front of me,
Hard body of the slums,
Hard mind of the street.
He has his two front teeth missing,
When he grins
His face resembles a splintered fence.
He has spots on his cheeks
Dope in his eyes
Murder on his fingers
(Not in his heart)
Only 'mom' in his heart.
On his shoulder a purple sore
That draws me in
Fascinated:
On his forearm his true
Love etched into his flesh
With a rusty switch
He thrusts
And his cock bounces joyfully
Against the satin finish
Of his black Adidas shorts,
To the muffled disco beat
He strips,
And grins
And you've just got to love him.
And he juts his hips towards you,
A five dollar bill tucked into the elastic waistband
Of his black Adidas shorts:
Bringing you a Latin word of love in your ear
And perhaps a sloppy kiss if you're over forty
And loaded:
It worries me,
I got the sloppy kiss, the word of love.
He sits
Legs apart on a small stool
To remove his cheap trainers,
His grubby white socks.

He grins and rubs his crotch,
The over forties go wild
With the five dollar bills.
He removes his shorts,
His dick is average
And refuses to harden,
He tugs it, twangs it
Pulls it and pummels it:
It died!
The (lucky) few at the front
Get to gum it,
Slurping and spitting it.
The Puerto Rican gogo boy dances on
To 'Call Me' by Blondie,
To 'Disco Inferno' by the Tramps.
I follow the tracks up his arms
To gaze at the purple sore.
The torso a tight washboard,
A steaming ploughed farm field;
The muscles gold and defiant.
He loves his work.
Afterwards ten dollars buys you a private show.
His name is Roberto.

III Magda-Sade

At Hellfire
Lining up the boys
Is Magda-Sade supplying the joys,
Each in turn she takes to blow
Twenty young men come and go:
Kleenex out to wipe the tips,
A moistened cloth to freshen the lips
Pops the bits into her bag
Never bites never gags.
Breasts so white as worthless tripe
Stomach sag and cellulite.
Dugs that droop
And flaps of clap,
She rules this Hell
She cuts the crap!

IV The Adonis

No Adonis
In the Adonis Lounge
Only the terminal
Only the lonely
They come
They go
They shuffle
They stalk
They loiter
They jerk
They sit in the toilet cubicles with the door open,
They sleep
Creep
Look shifty, act crazy.
They wipe their hands on the weed green velvet curtains
(But I never see them wash them)

V The Locker Room Party

6.30
Sunday afternoon,
A party
At the Locker Room
Tubs of grease
And paper towels
In the warmth
Of New York's bowels.
Dirty floors
And dirty talk
Watch the puddles
Where you walk.
Sweat and amyl,
Coke and cum
Crowded corners
Fun for some.
Bearded bodies
Handsome hands
With likewise souls that understand.
The sensual
The greedy bliss
Reddened eyes,
And mists of piss;
But watch out!
Don't make any slips
Here its strictly
Lips
Above the hips!

VI Yo Fucker Die

'Yo'
The crack addict
Follows me.
'Yo!
I said Yo!
Don't get nervous man,
Let's take a walk!'
The crack addict fastens to me
Like fire
He burns into me.
He's never gonna let me go.
'Slow down now.
Slow with me.
Watchoowant now.'
His eyes are the deep
Black Hudson,
Depth charges down there
Waiting to explode,
Waiting for a sign.
His are desperate words
Rasping with crack.
'Yo!
Whereyoufrom?
What's happenin' man?'
I walk on.
'Yo!
I said Yo hear me man!'
His shaking hand
Fastens round death
In his jacket pocket.
My knees kiss the sidewalk.
'Yo Fucker.
Die!'

VII Christopher Street Pier

There's a great pair of tits
On view,
And cocks the American way
Real big and thick and cut.
Big tits,
Big cock,
And all on one guy.
The pier is steaming this afternoon.
A gorgeous Puerto Rican girl
Plays with her hair,
Splays her legs
And winks at the sun.
A Honcho with a handlebar
Doesn't look twice:
He likes the big cut cocks,
He's got one of his own.
He couldn't give a dead donkey's dick
For the great pair of tits.

It's alive on the pier
In the slimy heat,
Today
(At the bottom of Christopher Street)
New Jersey Yahoos
Speed by in their boats.
'Ya Mutherfuckincocksuckinqueers man!'
This heat does things to the mind.

The water slaps the pier's ass
And a torso glides by
Arm waving out of the slimy water,
Twisting the clouds
Between the blue fingers:
(Like the strands of the gorgeous Puerto Rican
    girl's blue-black hair)
Then they see those tits.
'Jeezus Oohee!'
And who can blame 'em,
And as I smother in those
Fleshpots of wonder,
They crash the boat
And drown in the Hudson.
Mangled by the motor,
Their torsos glide by,
Arms a-waving,
Arms a-waving,
Fingers a-twistin'.
Bye Bye Fuckers
Ha Ha!

VIII After Dark

'I've had 'em all in here!
Sinatra said to me
He said
Jack he said
Jack
He said Jack
It's like this.
The biggest tip.
Real stars
Real
They don't make 'em like that
No more
No Sir!'

The taxi driver
Goes on and on
And on and on
Misses my stop
And glides into the park
After dark.

'Johnny Carson
Mean Mother
Gave me no tip at all,
With all his fuckin money man.
But Garland
She was a real star
Real
They don't make 'em like that no more
No Sir
Nope.'

After dark
At midnight
It's a full moon.
And the stars are out
Like we never used to see them.
(Maybe he sees the sweat on my brow)
'Yeah, she was great' I say,
'Can we go now?'

The Room Below (version)

I remember
When I lived
In a room, down in the basement
Below a brothel.

All night the girls would clump
Downstairs
In heavy platform shoes
I painted all the walls
In a wild flamenco orange,
One window in the doorframe
And the drains were always blocked.
Single bed pushed in the corner
Cigarette burns on the cover,
And the soft silky music
Cocooned me from the snow.
I was happy then,
Didn't know any better then;
My first time moved away from home
And there of course were you.

I would talk about childhood
And you talked about your paintings.
The electric fuse blown again,
We drowned our cold in wine
And we met across a candle,
And found something secure and special;
And later in a single bed
Our lives changed that night.

I remember
When I lived
In a room, down in a basement
Below a brothel.
And the guy upstairs
Would piss each morning
In the kitchen sink;
It leaked out from the rusty pipes
And trickled down the kitchen wall
But I was happy then
I didn't care at all.
Sometimes I felt lovely
And you brightened me with stories
Of a million dreams and glories,
They shimmered with your laughter
And glowed within your eyes.

I remember
When I lived
In a room
Below a brothel.
The footfalls marked the silent time,
For me each winter night.
We'd raise our heads from making love,
And listen to the sounds above
I was happy then
But there of course was you.
I moved out, owing all my rent:
To rooms of better light and space
I never saw that place again
And lost all track of you.

I think about the winter nights
When snowfall keeps me trapped inside
I wonder how you lived your life
And if you thought of me.
I think of how the candle lit
That room below
A brothel.

Oh! How I love Carmen Amaya
She sings my sad then happy heart
How I loved my kind of love
And you the love of art.

The Tijuana Kitchen

Perched on a red ripped barstool
At the Chile bar.
Eating the sort of food
That you suffer with twice.
Trying to stop an old guy
From digging in his spoon:
Feel your guts a-grumble
As you start to pay the price.
Ribcage in the soup
That doesn't look like chicken
Though it says so on the menu
And the waiter swears it's true.
Spits upon the table
And wipes it with his cloth
Wants to make it all fine
Home from home for you.
There's something in my coffee
That doesn't look so right
Forked it out with a coffeespoon
And watched it expire;
Legs up in the air
It passed on
Without a care.
Meat, just like the rubber
From a pick-up truck tyre.
You said you'd meet me lunchtime
In the Kitchen Tijuana.
And I know I said
That I'd do anything
For you,
But I'm sitting here a-suffering
And you haven't shown anyhow
Some things just aren't forgiven,
So I'm, telling you,
We're through!

King Fingers

He pushes his fat fingers
Into stretch rubber gloves,
He's got to dig in deep
If he wants to search for drugs.
You can hear the boy a-screaming
As the finger finds its mark
He can go at him all night
But he'll never make him talk.

Feet about a foot apart
Call me 'Sir' you bum
Pulls out a rubber finger
And pushes in a thumb
Rummage round a little while
'Nope Sir not a thing'
Pulls out his shitty fingers
Feeling like a king?

Beautiful Junkyard

Oh beautiful junkyard
You're the scrapheap of my heart,
Lean and ever hungry
You're a walking work of art:
Proverbial dark horse
In a cloud of mystery,
Oh beautiful junkyard
You're the rubbish tip of me.

My Fateful Love

Trouble waits on near horizons.
Eyes crackling like a storm,
Send me down a bolt of thunder
To keep me warm:
The fingers of some ghastly hand
Await
To grab me at the gate,
To test me of my faith in love
My love of faith.
My fateful love.

Saint Judy

Saint Judy
She's staggering across the floor
Saint Judy
Behaving like a whore
Saint Judy
She's giving it all the tears
She tears her dress
Looks a mess
Well I've wanted to do it for years
Well I've wanted to do it for years

Now I had a dream
Well, more a fantasy
Kip Noll, John Holmes and me
All in bed we were going O.T.T.
What a sight to see
What a sight to see

Well a diva a day
Keeps the boredom away
I love 'em when they throw up their arms
And bathe in that applause
Shouting
Screaming
Singing
Stamping
Slamming hotel doors
Champagne chilled
And the pills well spilled
All wide eyes
   (and overkill)

Minks
The drinks
The curves
The kinks
Always acts before she thinks
Well that's what you call a star boys
That's what you call a star

Too many of my skeletons
In other people's closets
Too many people taking without
Leaving deposits
Too many people bringing me down
Bringing me down

Well they may find me on a hotel floor
High heels, in a pool of gore
Curtains closed
And a bolted door
Breaking every law

And if I die before I wake up
I pray the Lord don't smudge my make-up
The dress will be fine when the hem
I take up
The dress will fit just fine

Sometimes I feel like a moral-less child
Sometimes I feel that I've gone too wild
Spilled my guts
Done myself in
Died for a multitude of sins
It feels so good to die for your sins
It feels so good
So good boys

Well let's all put on our sequinned dresses
And end it all in tears
Let's all holler and beat our breasts
Ending it all in tears
Christ I've wanted to do it for years

Saint Judy
What are we going to wear?
Saint Judy
Our souls we're going to bare
Saint Judy
She's squeezing out those tears
She tears her dress
Looks a mess
Christ I've wanted to do this for years

Hallelujah! Come on get happy!
You've gotta chase all your cares away
Hallelujah!
Come on get happy
We're waiting for the judgement day.

The Hustler

Over there
In the cold
Stands the hustler
His eyes are old
He has seen a million ugly scenes.
Places where men droop with mould,
The backrooms,
Where soiled goods are sold;
Seen with open eyes since frail fifteen.
He found it hard at first
But on his brow there sits a curse,
For when the young must suffer
At the hands of men.

Memories of Christmas past
Were never there to ever last,
Things as were can never
Be again.

Over there
By the wall
Stands the hustler
He's not very tall,
He's trampled by the jaded
By the sly.
He's seen the darker side of men
First fascinated and then
He found his urge to laugh
An urge to cry.
He'll find close friends
No friends at all,
He feels so lonely, tired and small
How few are chosen from
The golden call.

Memories of Christmas past
Were never there to ever last,
Things as were can never
Be again.

There's something in us all it seems
To crave adventure,
Hunt for dreams:
But corruption, the seducer, spoils
   our schemes.
As surely as the snow will melt,
The hustler
Grabs his soul, and heads for home
With lessons
Learnt under his belt.

Over there
By the wall
Stands the hustler
With the men of law,
On either side to flank the sallow youth.
But some of us will never learn
It takes the blow of fists to burn
How painfully we suffer
For the truth.

The Mamba

And tonight,
The look that branded me
Was like a pool,
Burnt out gasolene.
Shiny brown skin
Like the melting tar
On summer roads.
Finger on the trigger,
Words like bullets blast the brain;
Nails the brittle edge
Of a broken glass,
In a bar-room brawl.
Like myself
Like a jack rat,
Limp and lazy
On the sorrow-soaked floor.
Now you're feeling sorry
And I'm shattered,
Sad and worn out, ragged
Raped of mind and soul
Soiled as an ashtray,
Damp and dirty,
Grimed and greasy.
A broken-hearted effigy.
A bone-cracked
Cranium, face
Frozen up at you.

The cheap wine that
Drowned the demon in your brain
Has stained your mouth
And left a purple trail
Down heartache lane.
Slashing sickly senses
Leaving me in Hell.
The silent sob of shaking shoulders
As the candle drips and dies,
Drives out the tear-smeared figure
That I used to know as you.

Your heel grinds out the cigarette stub
You used to know as me.
Take a sip from the dirty glass
That helps to glitter up
Your dirty little life.
Loneliness may eat me up,
Keep determined
To survive;
And skin like cocained
Numb and yellowed
Cut with poison's pain.
Feeling, hot and shocked and shamed
The hero, that's the heroin
Helps me mellow out again:
And close my eyes in ecstacy
Cleansed from decaying crimes
That are sinking me
In self-pity.

Meet my eyes in a fired goodbye
Like a flicknife in the chest.
Just a tiny touch of you
So dark and damned and easy
Hope felled the prey
To a thousand use 'em, abuse 'ems.
For I know
That in the end
The poison darts
Of hate will rise,
From my oily sea
Of waxy lazy gloom,
That sends you spinning
In humiliation from the room.
And I know you,
Though you play at Dietrich in the bar
Slinking slurring out of key
Like some rank and jaded star.
But the colour seems to fade
Like the faked fur
You surely are.

You're much more Blue than Angel
Say goodbye to style and pride,
As you show your heart
As the knotted little organ,
That beats out
The number on the knees.
The sensuality
Of your glorious diamanté dress
That's hanging off your shoulders
Baring your bruised and battered chest,
As you beat out the rythm of the songs:
The rythm of the flesh
Singing 'Einen Mann'.
Qualluded, deluded,
Never, not for you.
And though you play at cat and mouse
By giving me your whisky mouth
Remember that
This little snake
Kisses you to kill,
And I'll buy them all a drink to toast
And charge the bill to you.
You'll never see
A faster mover
Dart in for the attack
Slithered, coiled danger
A twisted belt of black.
Treacle runs from all your pores
The venom from the bite,
Revenge is sweet
And strikes,
Just like a mamba
Every night.

The Scum of Love

Let us bathe in the music
My love,
That spits blood.
The music
That's the scum of love.
The music
Evokes the sighs of the dying
This music
The beauty of babies crying
The Devil's overture,
Sodomy and solitude
Blasphemy,
The way you make love to me.
Sperming over my sickness,
My lies.
My laboured breathing.
The music
Of mutilation, of hate
Pretty hate, black candles, bile:
The smile
Of my final moments.

Don't sleep too deep
Mr Sandman may forbid you
Your sweet dreams
Don't sleep
Too still
I may be the cat
On your failing breath.

Oh! The beauty of the gun,
Mother
Lover
Sister, son.

Oh! The beauty of the gun
The beauty
Of the gun.

Oh! The beauty of the knife
Father
Brother
Husband, wife
Oh! The beauty of the knife.
The beauty
Of the knife?

The Barriochino

Where the day melts into dusk
Where the men are bold with macho:
And the women gold with musk
Hug the sea that fucks the sand.
The cathedral cries:
The moon expires.
Flamenco drips from glistening pores
As whores reach high
And snatch the stars
To braid their pimps as matadors.

The singers thrust
Gardenias blush

Crazies with hash-dusted eyes,
Turbanned, oiled, and clench-butted;
Tightrope trip across the squares
Dripping drugs, and flicking drink,
Painted nails
And faggot winged,
Cheer the beggar as she sings.
Heels spear up the dog shit,
Cats cringe as vermin forage:
Pavestones hum, guitars strum
At Bar Darling, Bar La Concha,
Their cock beats upon the belly:
Fountains come.

Rouge on the lips of well-heeled cunt.

Striking drain slime,
Fluttering boys,
Sea rot, and swollen sun:
Skull-faced moon,
Fishribbed, Gothic noon.
The Barriochino seethes
With dog-knived bitches:
Paint drips from dock blubber,
Cellulite and sucking tongues.

Aniseed, shit-footed, bristles and tit
Sugar drips into dream poison
Yellow and wound pus
Bloody bandages, catarrh
Thick smoky throats
Thick meat heads of cut dick
Ripped up oiled vaginas
And nudging into caved in thigh
Hot and prickly, shitty assed
Where the days dissolve into sleep
Where sleep sinks into alleys dark

In gaudy windows plastic melts;
Transistors scar the view.
Sinister tangoes,
Final cruel jewelled beauty,
Dark beauty:
Eyes of a girl
Lips of a girl,
Cruel beauty everywhere.

The scarred breasts of Brazil
Ripped bellies of bulls
Lost limbs
Of the soldiers
Hacked fingers of thieves
Twisted spines of cripples
Raw asses of rent boys
Tainted lips of whores
Syphilitic tips of dicks
Ricketed knees of beggars
Unable to stand:
All in silver, gold, red and lace;
Brushed with fans and seductive smiles,
Rich with decay, the acidic sea
Eats the walls and strips the bones.
A galleon heaves in sleep,
Sharks rip Kodaks from
Fat Yankee necks,
Gums suck dick to the roots:
And the sun turns arms, smack brown,
Opium blushed and touched with dew.

The cathedral cries:
The moon expires.
Flamenco drips from glistening pores
As whores reach high
To snatch the stars
To braid their pimps as matadors.

Pushin' Ink

(for Spring)

There is a story on his arm
A secret on his chest,
A lover gone upon his thigh
A threat upon his ass:
Detailed scrolls of winding ink,
Like tendrils round a tree.
Declarations, observations,
Gleaming mysteries;
A wicked dagger, slim and sharp,
That pierces skull, and rose.
Deathly symbols,
Love's sweet signs;
A treasure map for one who knows.
A curl around a nipple
A spear through a shoulder blade,
Two pulsing hearts, a diving swallow,
Anchors, ace of spades.
Needled threaded reminders
Bravura crafted on the flesh,
A serpent in the crevices,
Writhing where it's wet.

Paintings for his lifetime
Decorations for parade;
A carpet for the Devil,
Coloured from the shades
Of Hell.
Vermilion slashes purple,
Bruised turquoise, indigos,
A plumage for a cockatoo:
Comfort for all self-adoring matelots
He wears them like his medals:
They tell stories of his wars
Evocative, provocative,
They forbid him Heaven's doors:
And for this he may be thankful?
Halos would never suit him well;
For he follows a trail of blood and ink,
To join all his friends
In Hell.

Star - I

Names do not cross
Though tongues entwine.
Those old, cynical, desperate:
Spit on their fingers
Yellow, mysterious oysters
   between finger and thumb
Drop like wax from a limp
   expiring candle.
Those with blind hope in their eyes
Attempt clumsy introductions
They are hurled into fusty corners
Where the moon sleeps
   for a hundred years:
We leave our shapes
   in this void
Entwined with others' noise
   in an endless web
That creeps its way from
   orgasm to sleep.
Silent choreography
A black dance
From hip to lip, to the grave.
Snails have traced across my jacket,
And my eyelids glitter
   from black flies.
The ritual is all,
Without conclusion;
Shuffling from one to another
   to another
To me......but no!

The cleansing seductive smell of mentholyptus
Clears my bursting temples
Opens my nostrils
To pave the way for sourer scents.

I am melting
Thawing, as ice
Droplets forming around the mouth
Glistening at the thigh,
Shapeless, amorphous,
I am taking the waters of youth,
A peasant at the well:
The dark shapes me into
    the ones I desire
That I shall be desired by
    ones such as me.
The dream shifts.
I am the dream
They come,
They make their offerings
They vaporise:
Sometimes they stay longer.

Star - II

In the circus
In the square
We are part
Of a cryptic ritual,
His eyes are
Like ochre-marbled eggs,
Forlorn, like a scolded hound.
He moves one up
The stained blood velvet cinema seats,
His stare in mine
Unfaltering
Watery, pleading
Sorrowful pools of nicotined years,
Meet mine
Darting to him,
The screen,
To him
The screen
To him
His charred coarse hand
Brushes me
(Trembling, though sure in its desperation)
Hesitation,
Confirmation,
In my ears a choir of black angels
Pulling me across scarlet,
To a musky warmth.
Slobbering alcoholic kisses
A stink of rotten cloth
And dead fish
On his fingers.

Mine is not the longing for tenderness.

Across a world of flaming might have beens,
Blunt blades, public shit,
Rubble, rot and moving garbage,
Laboured.
He has a strange glared look
Of desire, on the threshold of murder:
To murder
For that desire to meet its end.

I sink
Sweaty, under a sick humidity
Of body, piss and the untold.
Hungered,
Slimed with a score of spent agonized moments,
He puckers a kiss
It hits silence.
He gestures
To move to more dangerous corners,
I rise, slowly,
Weighted with the guilt of the sins of a city:
I am drawn,
Commanded
By this sorrowful, fetid being
Who is used to the command or curse
From one such as I.
For he has looked into
    my all revealing eyes,
And seen the truth in my
    lusting heart,
And he knows he is the one:
Outcast as maybe,
To nuture and still
    that greedy raging desire.

Who is slave or master?
The roles are blurred,
But at the core of this diseased heart
Pulses the one warm totem
That entwines our lives:
A world, a language, a generation
  a colour,
    apart.
Forever he is of my life
And I of his,
My dreams will search him out
And guilt will find him
Crouched over a fire,
Smouldering against a bleak winter sunset,
Or rotting in a mortuary
With vagrant on his tag:
For death had brushed him
And I,
For I suffered the pain of his
Tremulous touch:
A befouled raven
That sweeps and weeps
  its way
Through my daylight nightmares.

My cold overeager hand on
His black leathered heavy cock
Making welts
Wringing it numb
Pressing it against his swollen stomach
Torturing its spurts
Covers his hairless navel,
Spewing,
Making his knees buckle
Under the euphoria
Of waves of light
(From Heaven and Hell)
Twisted, as it hangs
Exhausted against the
   slicked inside of his dark
   bristled leg
   it swings, laboured
Like a blackened bull
Choked in the dusts
   of a burning storm,
   burning circle of sand,
In slow motion,
It swings
Like a ship's bell,
The death toll
On a doomed ocean liner;
Dark ship
Sinking
Whilst down below the
   crated cargo dislodges with the swell.

Star - III

From the womb
Wet and anointed,
Slippery as a calf, half born,
Hanging from the quivering guts:
(Not anticipating)
Impending misery.
To the slaughterhouse.

Star - IV

The Star
Moribund
Stumbles the path
Of strewn valium,
Crunching into the pile
Of beige hotel carpet.
He walks a marked path
To the bloodied bathroom
Where hands have told their frenzied anguish
On the white tiles
In red.

Send me black dahlias:
A bucket of spit
To moisten the slick of your thighs.
Sorrows, tears and darkness
To colour my song of sighs.

Poor Cherubin!
Slashed and razored
From the rays of God's halo:
Brutalized by aquiline jaw
El Auria
Under a dramatic curtain of stars
Eyes of a girl
Lips of a girl

Blood-curdling promises
Broken in a moment's guilty desire.
Thief of the key
To my heart.
Bastard of the Life of Lies
Laughing in the face of fate:
From the earliest hours of my life
Powerless,
To the end
To the place where visions are withheld
Where age claims you
And beauty withdraws
To the darker corners of the face.
To this wasteground where we still communicate:
Where no one understands
A fateful liason
Of you, you were, and you to be:
Loyalties, true to self.

In your miasma of desire
Mephistopheles broods
At your shoulder
Hardness takes root in your heart:
Crystals are formed.

You are radiant in ruination
Ordained in disease
Caressed with corruption
Kissed by the sins of the world
Victim of our sickening times
Sick cities
Decaying estates......

......Then a dawning
Cold vicious, radiant,
Like a dawn after a night's un-sleep;
That I may be the evil-
I, the one they move from,
Move to,
Oblivious or knowing
In the acceptance of death,
Where life holds no rich promise,
I may be the Evil.

The Star
Stands cornered,
A match illuminates:
   (the space)
Faces shrink into the walls,
Features implode,
The Star
Stands accused
Of being the Star:
The glimmering fading star
Astride the ugly,
At odds with, in amongst
The desperate
Sad star
Moves with a mantle of invisibility
He is fooled
But fools no one
That he is
The Star.
Fear rips the shoulder muscles
Flays the back
   with its prickly heat.
He is as them
(But not as them)
Because they are them
And he is the Star.
But being there in the midst of them,
The Star
Is dimmed
And becomes a cinder;
That is, one of them.

The room crumbles with laughter
Booths hiss with secrets and whispers,
Amongst the moaning.
A hush,
As quiet as ash.
The Star
Sinks back to the brick
Ash on brick:
The breath will dust it away.
And the silence is real.
Reality fills the head
Already cluttered with stars.
Filthiness pervades,
Reality prevails,
Lives cross,
The Evil is sealed
The moment of reality
Is sealed:
Until from the
Silent orifice
A scream that sears.
Are you the Star?

Somewhere in a city
    in a precinct
    in a street
    in a building
    in a corridor
    in a basement
    in a room
    in a corner
    in a moment
Reality twists
    and ash scatters.

The star
Implodes.
A leg becomes a torso
  becomes an arm
  becomes a head
  becomes a mouth
  becomes a cock
  becomes a hand
  becomes an arm
And a chain of sad stars
Stretch from the creeping
  West Side
To the bombsites of the Bronx.

I cry for the evil within me
And I close my eyes
And cry inside:
Cry
For the evil in my ruptured soul
That makes me
The Star.

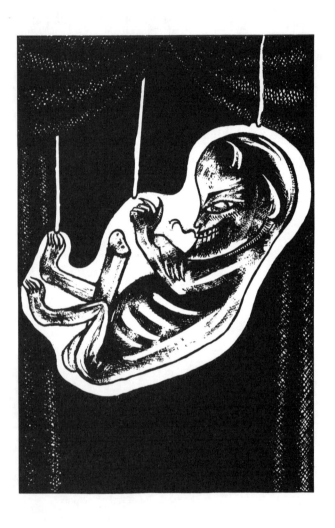

Unborn Stillborn

In the pulsing of the womb
Waits the unborn Prince of Evil:
Eyes ablaze with the light of unchained anguish seething.
Waits and bides timeless time to rip open vibrant stillborn
Crying
Help me to tear free like a wolf
In the night bays hungry.
Slides his tongue across grim and grinning teeth.
He moves in the night
With shadows,
Smiles as friend,
Touch as lover too.
He takes him the child to kiss him.
There's a curtain coming down over memory,
And silent, the stage glares empty;
And the blood tide, on the bitter shore,
Sweeps over the mind till morning.
I will never love again.
I will never ever
Love Again.

Gay Verse from GMP — The Gay Men's Press

NOT LOVE ALONE
Martin Humphries(ed)
Anthology of gay verse by 30 modern gay poets
ISBN 0-85449-000-0
144 pages UK £3.50/ US $6.50

DREAMS AND SPECULATIONS
Poems by
Paul Binding & John Horder
ISBN 0-85449-039-6
64 pages UK £2.95/ US $5.95

SO LONG DESIRED
Poems by
James Kirkup & John McRae
ISBN 0-85449-038-8
64 pages UK £2.95/ US $5.95

THREE NEW YORK POETS
Poems by
Mark Ameen, Carl Morse & Charles Ortleb
ISBN 0-85449-052-3
96 pages UK £3.95/ US $7.95

TONGUES UNTIED
Poems by
Dirg Aaab-Richards, Craig G Harris,
Essex Hemphill, Isaac Jackson &
Assotto Saint
ISBN 0-85449-053-1
96 pages UK £3.95/ US $7.95

GMP books can be ordered from any bookshop in the UK, and from specialised bookshops overseas. If you prefer to order by mail, please send full retail price plus £1.00 for postage and packing to GMP Publishers Ltd (M.O.), P O Box 247, London N15 6RW. (For Access/Eurocard/Mastercharge give number and signature.) Comprehensive mail-order catalogue free on request.

In North America order form Alyson Publications Inc., 40 Plympton St, Boston, MA 02118, USA.

****

PLEASE SEND MAIL-ORDER CATALOGUE TO:

Name..

Address ....

....

....

....